# Flying Power!

## Paper Airplanes & More

**CRAFT DESIGNER AND WRITER:**
**PHYLLIS DUNSTAN**

PUBLICATIONS INTERNATIONAL, LTD.

Phyllis Dunstan is a partner in a personalized design firm specializing in theme decorating. She is a member of the Peninsula Stitchery Guild and other craft organizations. Her creations have been seen extensively in national publications, including *Better Homes & Gardens, Redbook,* and *Good Housekeeping* and have appeared on numerous magazine covers.

Photography:
   Brian Warling Photography
Stylist and Technical Advisor:
   Lisa Wright
Models: McBlaine & Associates, Inc.:
   Melanie Magsaysay, Bobby
   Eubanks, Adam Bricker

Paper airplane formats © 1995 by Dennis Hommel Associates, Inc.

# CONTENTS

# INTRODUCTION

## DEAR PARENTS AND TEACHERS—

We know that most kids will be able to make these projects with little help, but there will be times when your assistance is needed. Occasionally, instructions direct the child to ask for adult help. You know your child's abilities—craft knives are very sharp and you should judge whether your child is able to handle one safely. Also, be sure everyone understands the "Important Things to Know!" section in this introduction.

Most important, this should be an enjoyable, creative experience. Although we provide specific instructions, it's wonderful to see children create their own versions, using their own ideas. ENJOY!

## HEY, KIDS—

With *Flying Power! Paper Airplanes & More* you can make any rainy day fun! This book will show you how to make out-of-this-world UFOs, dynamite dive bombers, fantastic flying saucers, and much, much more. Each one of these aircraft is fun to make and even more fun to fly. There is something for everyone in this book!

*Flying Power! Paper Airplanes & More* was made with you in mind. Many of the projects are fun things you can make by yourself. However, with some projects, you will need to ask an adult for help.

It's a good idea to make a project for the first time following the instructions exactly. Then, feel free to make another, using your imagination, changing colors, adding a bit of yourself to make it even more yours. Think of all the variations you can make and all the gifts you can give!

Most important, HAVE FUN! Think how proud you'll be to say, "I made this myself!"

## IMPORTANT THINGS TO KNOW!

Although we know you'll want to get started right away, please read these few basic steps before beginning:

1. Go through the book and decide what project you want to make first. Read the materials list and the instructions completely.

2. Gather all your materials, remembering to ask permission before you borrow something! If you need to purchase materials, be sure to take along your book or make a shopping list so you know exactly what you need.

3. Prepare your work area ahead of time. Cleanup will be easier if you prepare first! If a project calls for painting, make sure you cover your work surface with newspaper in case of spills.

4. Be sure that an adult is nearby to offer help if you need it. Adult assistance is needed if you will be using a craft knife or anything else that may be dangerous.

5. On patterns, dotted lines show you where to fold, while solid lines indicate where to cut. For neat folds, place a ruler by the dotted line and fold the paper over the ruler. Then remove the ruler and crease the paper with your fingernail.

6. Be careful not to put any materials near your mouth. Watch out for small items, like beads, around little kids and pets.

7. Wear an apron when painting with acrylic paints, because after the paint dries, it is permanent. If you do get it on your clothes, wash with soap and warm water immediately.

8. Clean up after you're done, and put away all materials and tools.

## FLIGHT INFORMATION

Out-of-doors is the best place for you to play with most of these aircraft—you don't want to break anything if you stay inside! Be sure you stay away from trees, the street, and electrical wires. If one of your toys lands on the roof or in a tree, leave it there and make another one. Also, *never throw a plane at anyone.*

Happy crafting!

# COME BACKER

WITH PRACTICE YOU CAN MAKE THIS COLORFUL BOOMERANG FLY AWAY FROM YOU AND THEN COME RIGHT BACK.

## WHAT YOU'LL NEED

4 foam plates, 9-inch diameter
3 sheets craft foam, 3 different colors

**Tools:** compass, scissors, craft glue

**1.** Use a compass to draw a 5½-inch circle on the bottom of each of the 3 foam plates and a 3½-inch circle on the fourth plate. Cut these circles out.

**2.** Using the compass, draw a 3¼-inch circle in the center of each of the 5½-inch circles. Use scissors to poke a hole in the middle of each plate. Be careful not to stab yourself! Starting at the hole, cut out the inner circles, making rings.

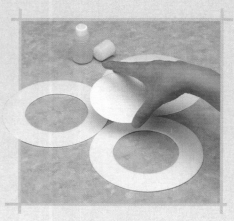

**3.** Arrange the 3 rings in a triangular position with their edges touching each other but not overlapping. Glue the 3½-inch circle (from Step 1) to the center of the 3-ring triangle. Set aside to dry.

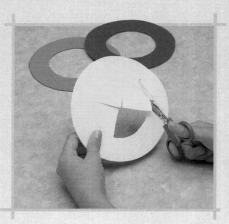

**4.** Using the compass, draw a 5½-inch circle on each color of craft foam. Cut out. Use the compass to draw a 4-inch circle in the center of each 5½-inch circle. Use scissors to poke a hole in the middle of each foam circle. Be careful not to stab yourself! Starting at the hole, cut out the inner circles to make rings.

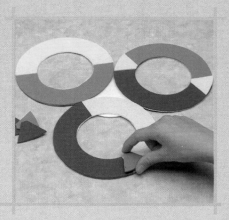

**5.** Cut each craft-foam ring in half and glue two halves to each of the white rings, mixing and matching the colors.

**6.** Use the triangle pattern on page 47 to trace and cut out triangles from leftover scraps of craft foam. Glue triangles over the edges where two ring colors are joined, using the color that is not already used on each ring.

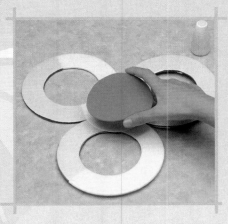

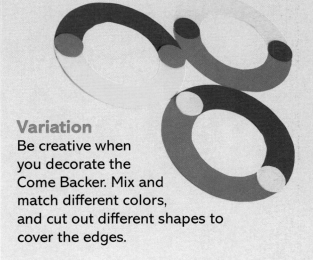

**Variation**
Be creative when you decorate the Come Backer. Mix and match different colors, and cut out different shapes to cover the edges.

**7.** Use the compass to draw a 3½-inch circle on one sheet of craft foam. Cut out the circle and glue it to the center circle on the back of the Come Backer.

## FLYING TIPS

Throw this boomerang using a sidearm motion, or place it on the edge of a book held in your hand. Flick your finger against the edge of the boomerang as hard and as fast as you can. It takes some practice in order to make the Come Backer fly out and then come right back to you, so keep trying!

# UFO Power Flyer

Greetings, Earthlings! This out-of-this-world UFO comes in peace!

## What You'll Need
2 plastic plates, 9-inch diameter
6-inch plastic bowl
10 black ¾-inch adhesive circle labels (or white labels colored black with felt-tip marker)
¾-inch red adhesive letters— U, F, O
Contact paper: red, blue
Gold adhesive star stickers in several sizes
**Tools:** scissors, craft glue

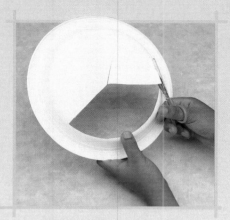

1. Use scissors to poke a hole in the middle of one of the plates (plate 1). Be careful not to stab yourself! Starting at the hole, cut out the middle part of the plate.

2. Apply a thin ribbon of glue to the outer rim of plate 1. Turn the second plate (plate 2) upside down and glue the 2 rims together. Allow to dry.

3. To make the "control room," turn the bowl upside down and stick circle labels around the side. Add adhesive "UFO" letters to the top (really the bottom) of the bowl.

4. Glue the rim of the bowl to the center of plate 2. Allow to dry.

## FLYING TIPS

Toss the UFO as you would toss a Frisbee flying disc.

5. Decorate the sides of the saucer with strips of blue and red contact paper. Scatter some stars on the sides and top as well.

# FA THUNDERHAWK

THIS KILLER FLYING MACHINE IS READY TO BATTLE FOR CONTROL OF THE SKIES! CARRYING TONS OF WEAPONS, THIS ATTACK BOMBER CAN DAMAGE ENEMY OUTPOSTS.

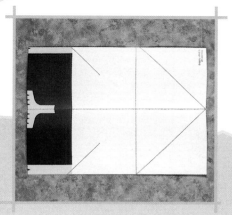

1. Fold the paper in half on the center line, and open up the paper so it lies flat.

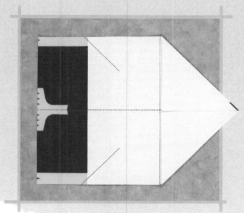

2. Fold down both corners.

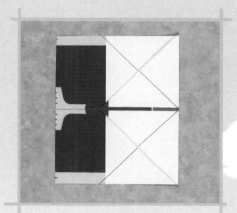

3. Fold down the tip.

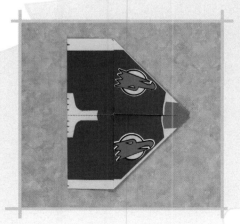

4. Fold down the corners again.

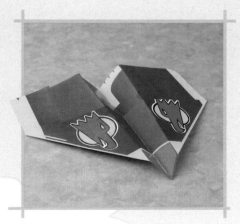

5. Fold the plane in half. Then fold down the wings one at a time.

**6.** Fold up both wing tips.

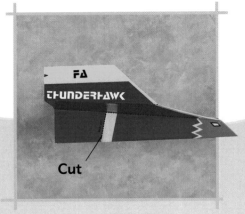

Cut

**7.** Cut the tail along the dotted cutting line.

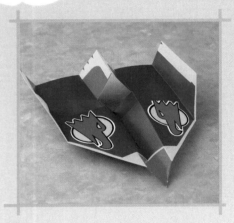

**8.** Fold up the tail, and shape the plane as shown.

# FLYING TIPS

Turn the wing tips up for loops, and turn them down for straight glides. The harder you throw the plane, the faster it will fly.

# SPINNER WINNER

It's awesome! Pull the string and watch the Spinner Winner whiz and spin through the air.

## WHAT YOU'LL NEED

6×6-inch lime green cardstock
Blue glitter glue pen
Small wooden thread spool
36 inches blue carpet thread
Magenta pony bead

**Tools:** Tracing paper, paper clips, pencil, ruler, carbon paper, scissors, craft knife, craft glue

*Have an adult help you when using the craft knife.*

1. Place tracing paper over spinner pattern on page 48 and secure with paper clips. With a pencil, trace over all lines, including the cutting and folding lines. Use a ruler to help you trace straight lines. Remove tracing paper from pattern.

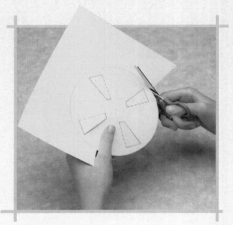

2. Place carbon paper between cardstock and tracing paper pattern. Paper clip the 3 together and trace over all lines to transfer the pattern onto the cardstock. Remove clips.

3. Cut the circle out, and ask an adult to help you cut the straight lines with a craft knife and ruler. Do not cut along the dotted lines—these are fold lines.

4. Decorate the spinner base using the glitter glue pen. Make sure you decorate both the top and bottom of the spinner.

**5.** Glue spool to middle of spinner. Let dry completely.

**6.** When glue is dry, fold along the dotted lines so the flaps bend up a little bit.

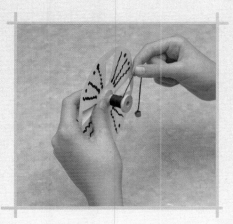

**7.** Tie bead to the end of the thread. Wrap thread tightly around spool.

## Variation

Instead of using glitter glue, you can use colored paper and a glue stick to decorate the spinner. You can also draw a design with felt-tip markers, use dimensional paint, or apply your favorite stickers.

## FLYING TIPS

Set the spool lightly on the pointed end of a sharpened pencil. Pull the end of the thread firmly and quickly. The Spinner Winner should go whizzing through the air. Watch what happens when you fold the flaps up more!

# ROCKET POWER

4...3...2...
1... Blast off!
You provide the
power to send
this rocket into
outer space. Ask
a friend to help
with the launch.

## WHAT YOU'LL NEED

Paper towel tube
Construction paper: yellow, red
Bright-patterned wrapping paper,
 7½×6 inches
Drinking straw
Red adhesive star stickers
25 feet red carpet thread
Craft stick
Small pony bead
Large balloon
**Tools:** ruler, scissors, compass, craft glue, tracing paper, paper clips, pencil, carbon paper, masking tape

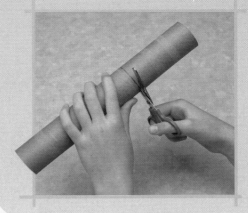

1. Cut paper towel tube to 7-inch length.

2. Use a compass to draw a 5½-inch circle on yellow paper. Cut out. Fold circle in half. Make a crease. Unfold. Cut along creased line.

3. Overlap the straight edge of one half of the circle to make a cone shape that extends ¼ inch beyond the tube's edge when it is placed on top of tube. Glue overlapped edges of cone in place. Discard the other half of the circle.

4. Apply a narrow ring of glue around top edge of tube. Place cone on top of tube, center it, and push excess paper down, smoothing it into glue. Let dry.

**5.** Turn wrapping paper face down and run a line of glue across the top edge and down **one** side. Lay tube on paper, lining up the top edges. Press glued edge of paper to tube, making sure it is straight. Roll tube across paper, applying glue to the tube as it rolls along.

**6.** Push the extra ½ inch of paper at the bottom to inside of tube.

**7.** Cut straw to 4 inches and glue it securely to the center of one side of the rocket. Allow to dry.

**8.** Cut a 1×6-inch strip of red paper. Use scissors to fringe one long side. Glue it around top edge of rocket under cone.

**9.** Add star stickers to the cone in a pleasing design.

**10.** Place tracing paper over fin pattern on page 47 and secure with paper clips. Using a ruler and pencil, trace over all lines on pattern. Repeat to make a second fin. Remove tracing paper from pattern.

**11.** Place a sheet of carbon paper between red paper and tracing paper pattern. Paper clip the 3 sheets together and trace over the lines to transfer patterns onto red paper. Remove clips. Cut out. Fold tabs on dotted lines.

**12.** Glue fins to the bottom of the rocket, placing them across from each other, with the straw centered between them.

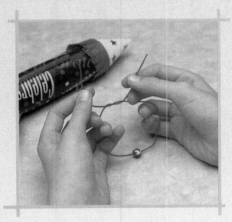

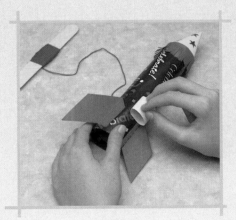

**13.** Wrap thread around craft stick. Thread loose end through straw from bottom to top. Slip bead onto thread and tie a loop large enough to go over a doorknob. Make sure the bead is in the loop.

**14.** Roll a 3-inch piece of masking tape into a loop, with the sticky side out. Stick the tape 2 inches up from bottom edge of rocket, on the side opposite straw.

## BLASTING TIPS

Blow up a balloon. Hold the stem and lay the fullest part of the balloon on the tape, stem end pointing to the back of the rocket. Stick the balloon securely to the tape and gently let the air out. Slip the loop of thread over a doorknob. Unwind the thread and give the end to a friend to hold. Slide the rocket up near your friend's hand. Holding on to the rocket, blow up the balloon. Have your friend hold the thread tautly and at a slight upward angle. When you are ready, release the balloon stem and give the rocket a slight nudge. It's blast-off time!

# WHIRLY BIRD

FUN TO MAKE AND EVEN MORE FUN TO FLY, THE WHIRLY BIRD TWIRLS THROUGH THE AIR LIKE A MINIATURE HELICOPTER.

## WHAT YOU'LL NEED

3×10-inch yellow cardstock
Purple adhesive stickers
**Tools:** tracing paper, paper clips, pencil, ruler, carbon paper, scissors

1. Place tracing paper over Whirly Bird pattern on page 47 and secure with paper clips. With a pencil, trace over all the lines, including cutting and folding lines. Use a ruler to help trace straight lines. Remove tracing paper from pattern.

2. Place carbon paper between cardstock and tracing paper pattern. Paper clip the 3 together and trace over all the lines to transfer pattern onto cardstock. Remove clips. Cut out. Make the three cuts as indicated on pattern.

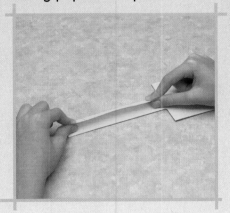

3. Fold section **C** forward and section **D** backward.

4. Fold **A** forward and **B** backward. Decorate with star stickers.

5. Bend the stem up at **E**.

## FLYING TIPS

Hold the stem upright with the flaps on top, and drop the Whirly Bird from a high place, such as the top of a staircase. Try tossing the Whirly Bird high into the air.

# HOVER CRAFT

THIS IS A FLIGHT THAT BARELY GETS OFF THE GROUND. YOUR FRIENDS WILL BE AMAZED AT THE WAY THE HOVER CRAFT GLIDES THROUGH THE AIR.

# WHAT YOU'LL NEED

5-inch square corrugated cardboard, ⅛-inch thick
Pop-up squirt-bottle cap
Purple acrylic paint
Binder reinforcements
Silver glitter glue
Large balloon

**Tools:** compass, pencil, scissors, craft knife, paintbrush

*Have an adult help you when using the craft knife.*

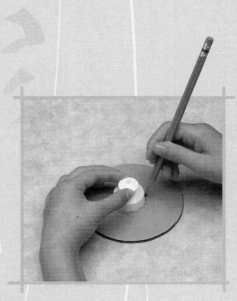

1. With a compass, draw a 4-inch circle on the cardboard. Cut out. Center the squirt-bottle cap on the cardboard circle and trace around it with a pencil.

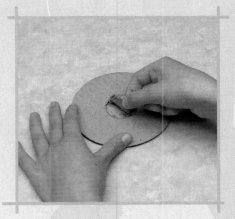

2. With the help of an adult, use the craft knife to cut out the center circle, cutting through the **top 2 layers of cardboard only**. Peel away these 2 layers of the center circle, leaving the bottom layer intact.

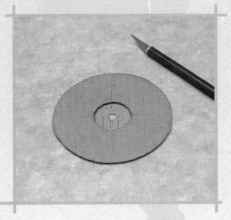

3. With the help of an adult, use the craft knife to cut a ¼-inch square hole in the center of the bottom layer. Push the bottle cap down into the circle. It should fit firmly and tightly. (Remove cap before painting and decorating the cardboard.)

23

**4.** Paint both sides of cardboard circle with acrylic paint, allowing paint to dry on one side before painting the other side. Let paint dry completely. Decorate the top of the Hover Craft with binder reinforcements. Add silver rays with glitter glue. Let dry.

**5.** Push bottle cap back into the center circle.

## HOVER TIPS

Blow up the balloon and, while squeezing the stem of the balloon to trap air inside, slip the stem over the bottle cap (be sure the cap is closed so air can't escape). Place the Hover Craft on a smooth, flat surface. Open the cap, give the craft a slight nudge, and watch it glide across the surface. The Hover Craft will glide more smoothly and for longer amounts of time if the balloon is centered directly over the bottle cap. This may take a little adjustment.

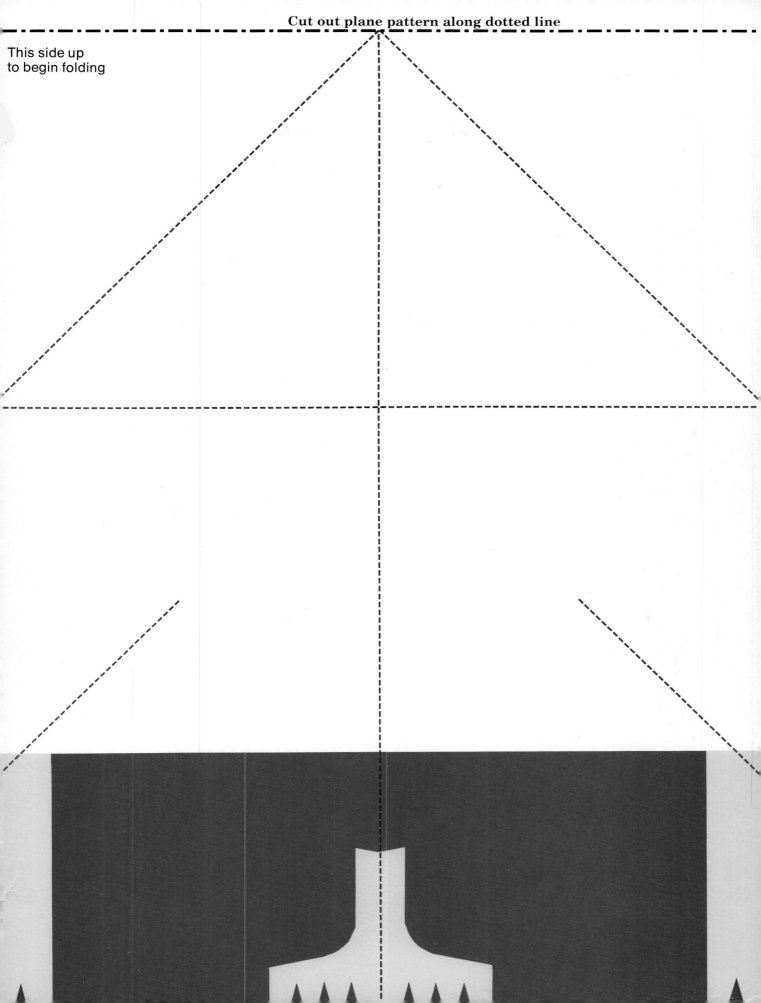

This side up
to begin folding

Cut out plane pattern along dotted line

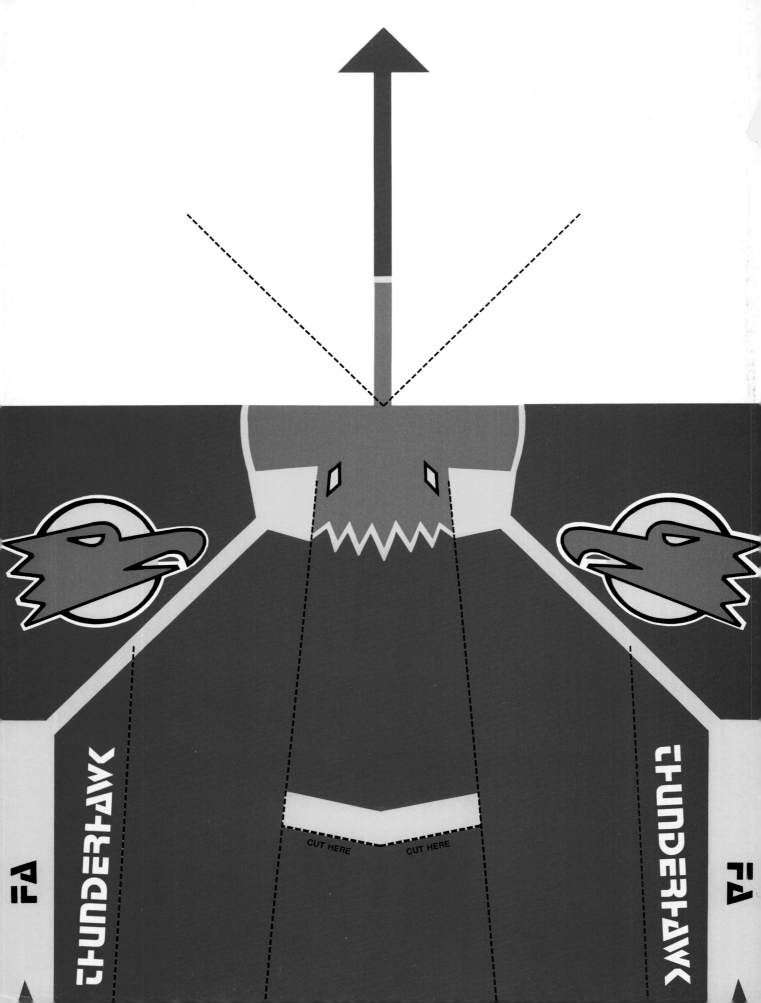

CUT HERE    CUT HERE

Cut out plane pattern along dotted line

CUT HERE

CUT HERE

This side up
to begin folding

TAIL

WING

Cut out plane pattern along dotted line

TAPE
PENNY
HERE

WING POSITION

TAIL POSITION

THUNDERDART

THUNDERDART

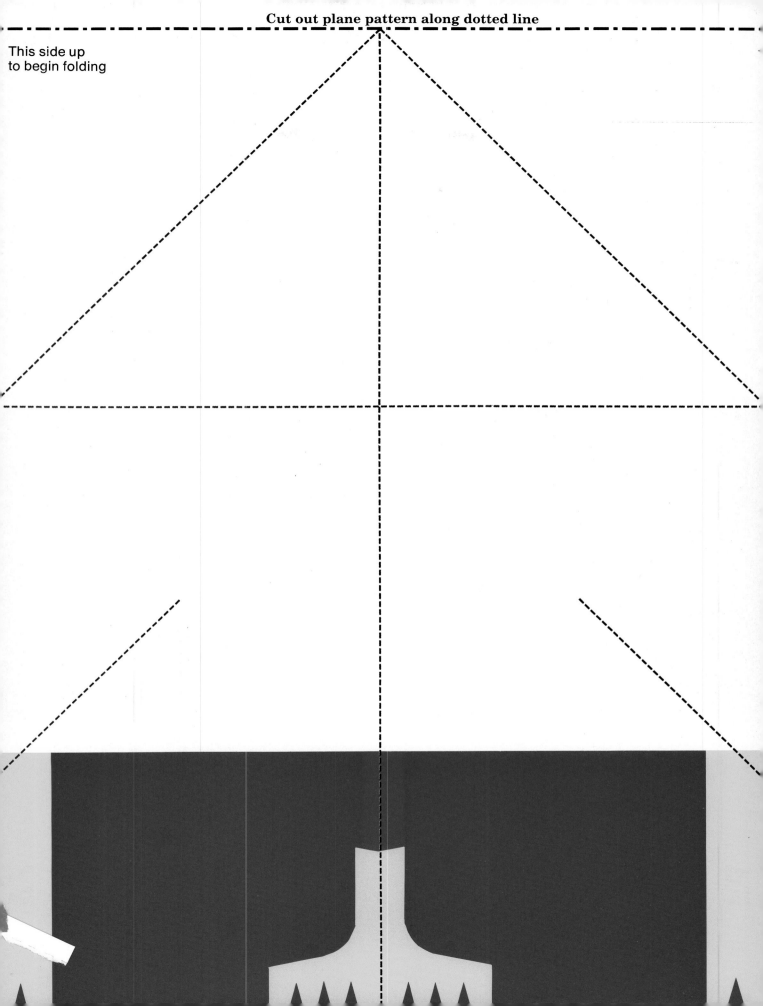

**Cut out plane pattern along dotted line**

This side up
to begin folding

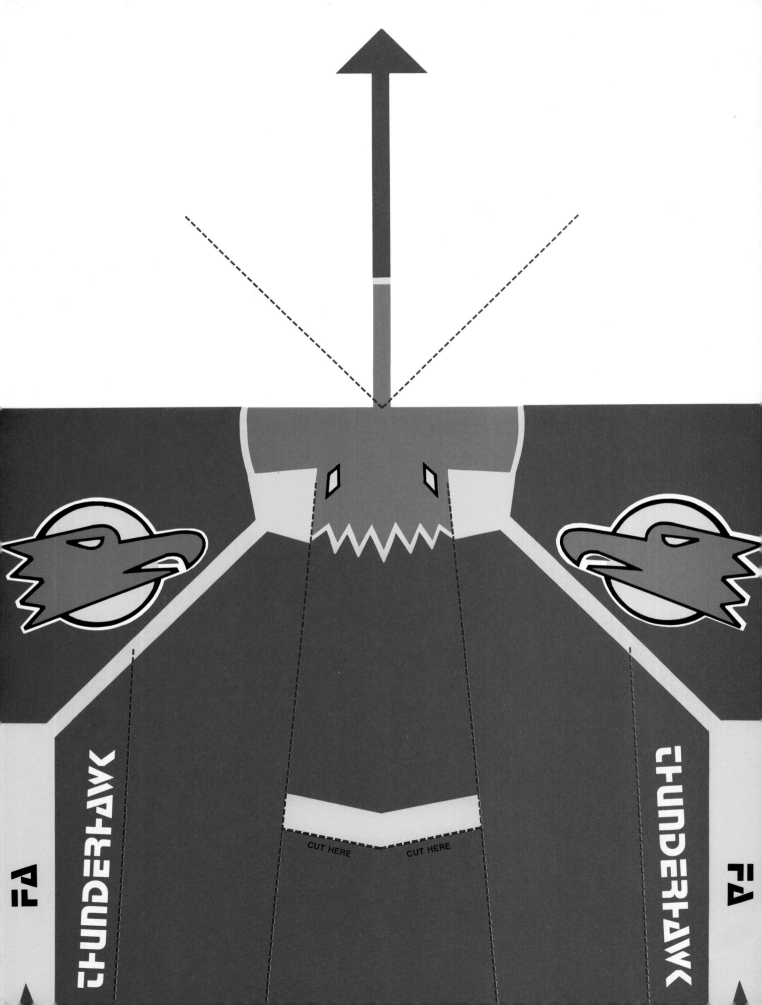

**Cut out plane pattern along dotted line**

CUT HERE

CUT HERE

This side up
to begin folding

TAIL

WING

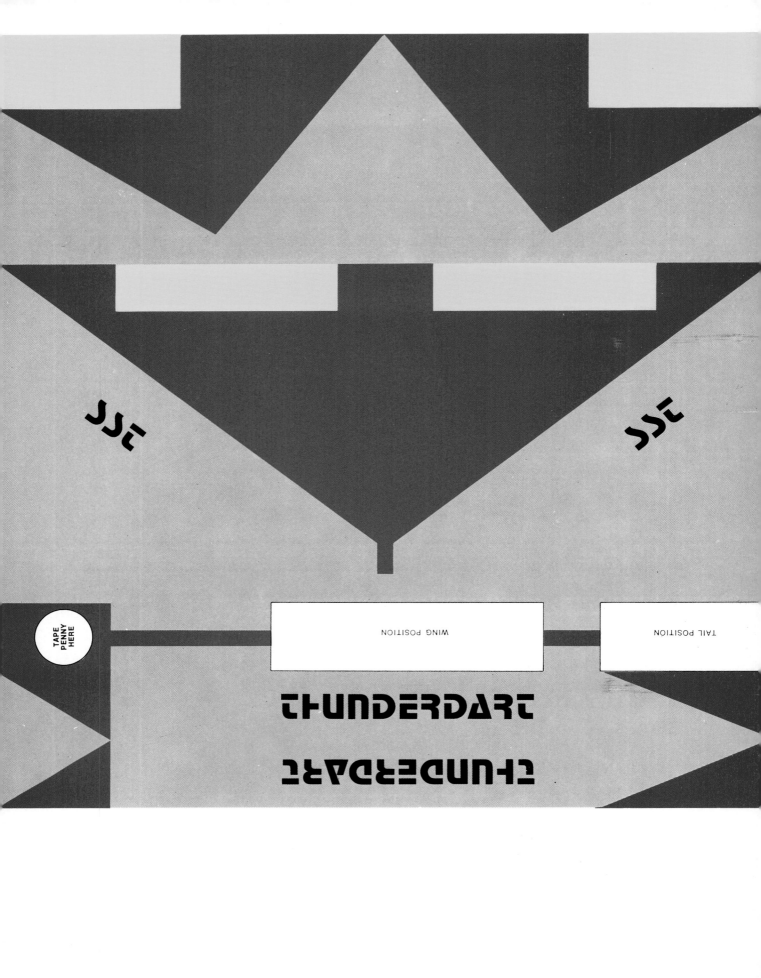

# SST Thunderdart

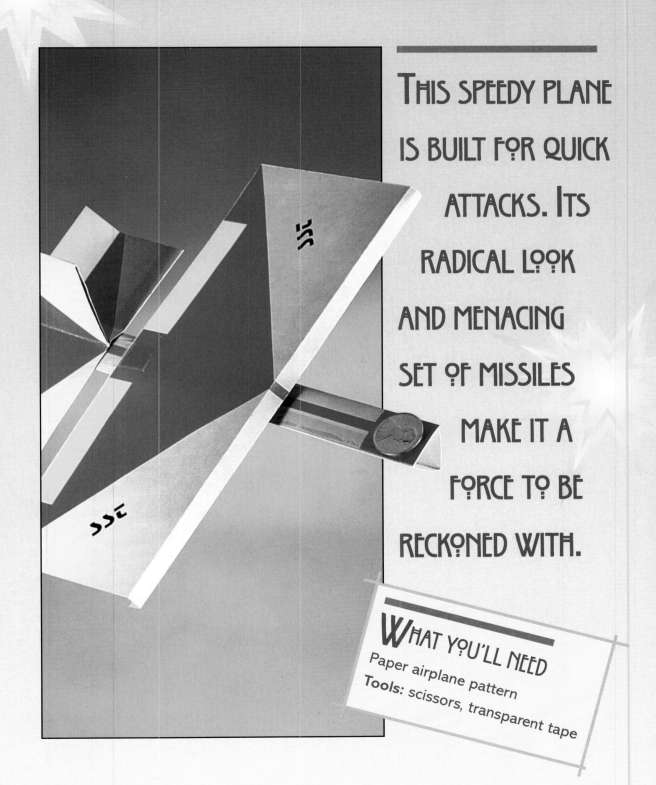

This speedy plane is built for quick attacks. Its radical look and menacing set of missiles make it a force to be reckoned with.

## What you'll need

Paper airplane pattern
**Tools:** scissors, transparent tape

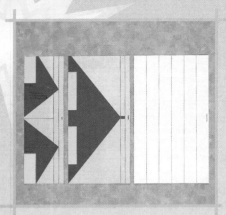

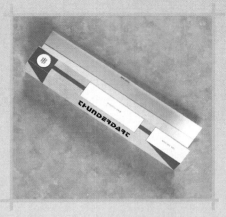

1. Cut apart the wing, tail, and fuse-lage (the plane's main body) along the cutting lines.

2. Fold up the fuselage along the fold lines.

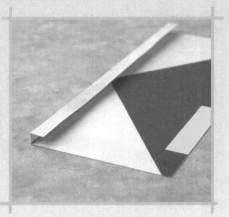

3. Roll the fuselage several times until it resembles a triangular tube, then tape it. Set aside.

4. Fold back the front edge of the wing twice so the edge forms a triangle.

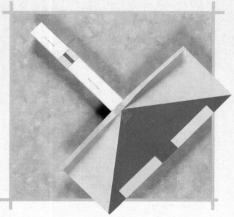

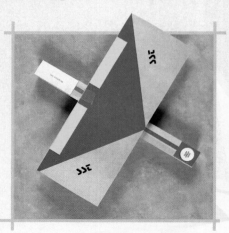

5. Tape the underside (belly) of the front folded edge of the wing to the fuselage.

6. Flip the wing back (toward the tail section) onto the fuselage, and tape the rear of the wing. Set aside.

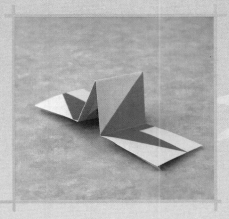

**7.** Fold back the tail's front edge once up to the second folding line. Then fold the tail in half, and fold up the tail "wings."

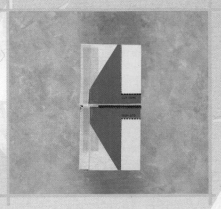

**8.** Turn the tail over, and place tape across the bottom.

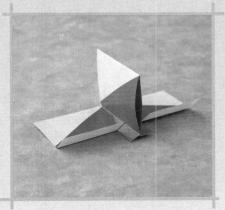

**9.** Cut and fold the tail flaps.

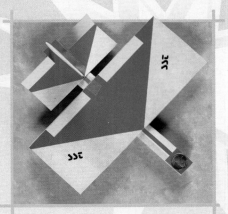

**10.** Tape the front of the tail to the fuselage. Roll up a piece of tape (sticky side out), and place it between the bottom of the tail and the end of the fuselage. Tape a penny to the top of the nose for added weight.

## FLYING TIPS

Start with gentle throws. Make sure the wing and tail are neat and even; add more tape if needed. For straight glides, raise the tail flaps very little or make them even with the tail. For high loops, raise the tail flaps, and throw the plane hard and upward a bit.

# Silver Wing

It's a bird! It's a plane! It's a Silver Wing! This sleek aircraft is bound to turn a few heads.

## What You'll Need

Clean foam meat tray
Silver acrylic paint
Adhesive stickers
8 metallic streamers, ¼ inch wide and 12 inches long
Paper clip or penny

**Tools:** scissors, ruler, pen, craft knife, paintbrush, transparent tape, craft glue

*Have an adult help you when using the craft knife.*

1. Trim off the curved edges of the meat tray, leaving the bottom flat with 4 straight edges.

2. Using ruler and pen, draw a triangle that stretches from the top of the rectangular meat tray to the bottom. Cut out. You will be left with 1 large triangle and 2 smaller triangles. The large triangle is the wing, and 1 of the small triangles is the rudder. Discard the other small triangle.

3. Draw a 3-inch line from the center of the bottom edge of the large triangle to the midpoint. Cut along this line to form a slot wide enough for another piece of foam to fit snugly into (about ⅛ inch wide). This is the wing slot.

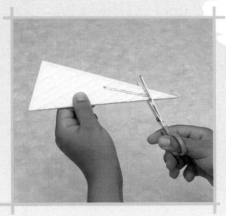

4. Cut the front of the smaller triangle off at an angle. This triangle will be the rudder.

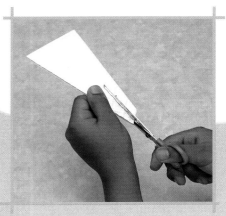

**5.** Draw a 2-inch line from the center of the slanted edge of the rudder not quite to the midpoint. Cut along this line to form a slot the same width as the wing slot.

**6.** Push the rudder slot into the wing slot with slanted edge of rudder facing up. The rudder should stick out about ½ inch past the end of the wing.

**7.** Remove the rudder and draw a fold line in it as shown. Set aside.

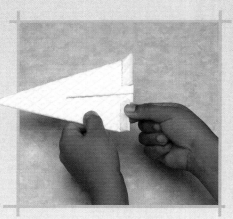

**8.** On the bottom edge of the wing, make a ½-inch-long cut on each side of the slot. Draw a fold line from each ½-inch-long cut out to the side of the wing. Fold the wing up at the fold lines. These flaps are called "elevators" and will help the Silver Wing glide smoothly.

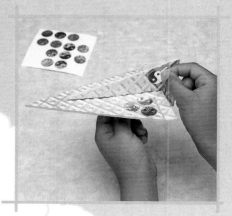

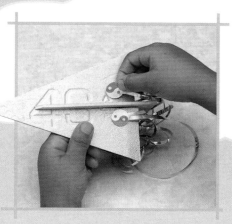

**9.** Paint one side of the wing and rudder with silver paint. Allow to dry. Turn both pieces over and paint the other side. Let dry completely. Insert rudder into wing slot. Decorate plane with stickers.

**10.** Tape the ends of eight 12-inch metallic streamers together in pairs. Attach the taped ends to the bottom of the wing on both sides of the rudder using a decorative sticker and some glue.

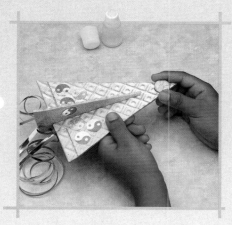

### Variation
Experiment with both a square and rectangular tray. Change the shape of the nose or the wing or round off the top of the rudder. Experiment with your own design to see what happens.

**11.** Tape a penny to the nose of the wing for weight, or add a paper clip. You can cover up the penny with a sticker if you wish.

## FLYING TIPS

Straighten the rudder and bend the elevators up slightly. Toss the Silver Wing in a gentle glide. If it dives to the ground, try moving the elevators up or use less nose weight. (The larger the Silver Wing, the more nose weight it needs.) Keep adjusting the elevators and nose weight until the Silver Wing glides to your satisfaction. It is important that both elevators are bent equally.

To make the Silver Wing turn to the right, bend the rudder flap right. Bend it left to make it turn to the left. Throw the Silver Wing straight ahead with force to make a loop.

# PARACHUTE PIZZAZZ

THIS PARACHUTE IS A BREEZE TO MAKE. AND THE HIGHER YOU THROW IT, THE LONGER IT WILL FLOAT.

## WHAT YOU'LL NEED

10×10-inch dark-colored tissue paper

Household bleach

4 sequins

4 pieces of thread, 12 inches long

Small, empty, plastic or wooden thread spool

Acrylic paint, dimensional paint, stickers, sequins, or other decorative items

Small weight (bead or metal washer)

**Tools:** bowl, craft glue, needle

*Make sure you are in a well-ventilated area when you make this parachute.*

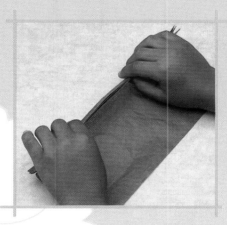

1. Fold the tissue paper in 1-inch accordion pleats like a fan.

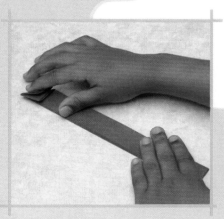

2. Fold this strip into triangular pleats.

3. Pour a little bleach into a bowl. (Wear a smock or an old shirt to protect your clothing from drips and splashes, and make sure your work area is well ventilated.) Dip just the tip of each corner of the folded triangles into the bleach. Remove tissue paper from bleach quickly.

4. Carefully unfold the tissue paper. Allow to dry.

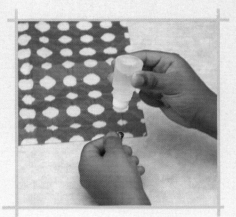

5. Glue a sequin on each corner of the tissue square.

**6.** Thread one piece of thread onto needle and make a tight knot at the end. Push the needle down through the center of one of the sequins and through the tissue, pulling the knot next to the sequin. Remove needle from thread and repeat the procedure with the remaining pieces of thread on the other 3 corners.

**7.** Decorate spool with acrylic paint, sequins, dimensional paint, or stickers.

**8.** Pull loose ends of the threads through spool and tie them around the weight.

### Variation

Use white tissue paper and pleat it the same way. Pour a little food coloring into a bowl and add a few drops of water. Dip the corners of the tissue into the food coloring. Try using a different color for each corner. You can also buy predecorated tissue paper in bright patterns if you choose.

## FLYING TIPS

To launch the parachute, hold it by the middle of the square and throw it up as high as you can. It will open up and float to the ground. Or, fold the parachute several times into a ball. Gather in the strings without wrapping them around the parachute. Toss it straight up and watch it float to the ground.

# A7 MOONRAIDER

TAKE OVER THE SKIES WITH THE A7 MOONRAIDER'S FEARSOME FLIGHTS. THIS IS THE HOTTEST PLANE EVER TO TAKE TO THE SKY.

## WHAT YOU'LL NEED

Paper airplane pattern

**Tools:** scissors, transparent tape

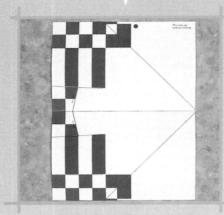

**1.** Fold the paper in half on the center line, and open up the paper so it lies flat.

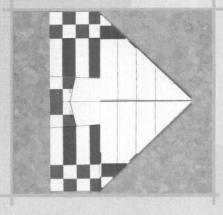

**2.** Fold down both corners.

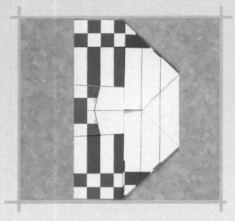

**3.** Fold back the tip on the first fold line.

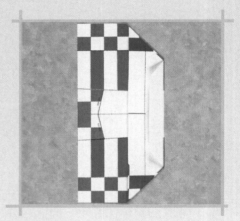

**4.** Fold back the tip a second time.

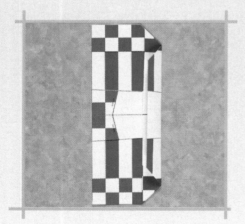

**5.** Fold back the tip a third time.

**6.** Fold the plane in half, and cut the tail along the dotted cutting line.

**7.** Fold the plane in half the opposite way.

**8.** Using the fold lines farthest from the wing tips, fold down the wings one at a time.

**9.** Fold up both wing tips. Tape the nose.

**10.** Push the tail through along the cut lines so it sticks up.

## FLYING TIPS

To make the plane loop and return to you, launch it slightly sideways and throw it in a slight upward direction. Throwing the plane straight ahead with the wings even with the ground will make it glide and "sputter."

# MINI BIRD KITE

THE BIRDS ARE
COMING! LET YOUR
IMAGINATION SOAR
AND MAKE A
WHOLE FLOCK OF
BIRD KITES.

## WHAT YOU'LL NEED

Lunch bag
Yellow acrylic paint
2 white binder reinforcements
Felt-tip markers: black, red
2 bamboo barbecue skewers
Black carpet thread
1 sheet pink tissue paper
3 pink feathers
Craft stick

**Tools:** tracing paper, paper clips, pencil, carbon paper, scissors, paintbrush, wire cutters, ruler, craft glue, tape

1. Place tracing paper over Bird Kite pattern on page 48 and secure with paper clips. With a pencil, trace over all lines. Remove tracing paper from pattern.

2. Place carbon paper between lunch bag and tracing paper pattern. Paper clip the 3 together, and trace over all lines to transfer pattern onto lunch bag. Remove clips. Cut out.

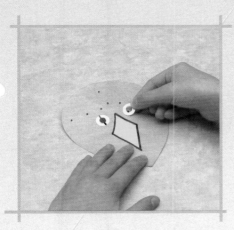

3. Paint beak yellow. Add 2 binder reinforcements for eyes. Outline beak with black marker and color in the center of the eyes.

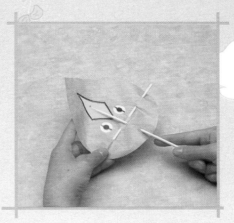

4. With the pointed end of a barbecue skewer, punch holes where marked. Thread the horizontal skewer through the holes first, and then thread the vertical skewer through. Use wire cutters to cut off the extra length of each skewer, leaving ½ inch on the bottom of the vertical skewer.

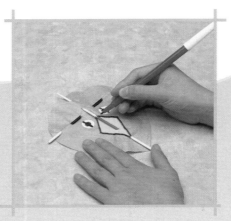

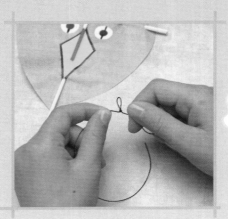

**5.** Use black marker to color eyebrows on the horizontal skewer and red marker to color the portion of the vertical skewer that lays on the beak.

**6.** Cut a piece of thread 16 inches long. Tie a small loop in the middle of the thread. Tie 2 more small loops, 1 on each side of the first loop, about ½ inch away. This thread is called the bridle.

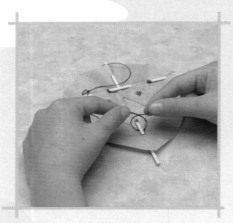

**7.** On back side of kite, tie one end of bridle to the skewer at the top of the kite. The center loop should be 3½ inches from top of kite. Tie the other end of the bridle to the skewer at the bottom of the kite so the center loop is 4½ inches from bottom of kite. Add a spot of glue to each knot on the skewer and trim away excess thread.

**8.** Cut several strips of tissue paper ½-inch wide. Tape these strips together to form a 6-foot-long tail. Tie a small loop of thread to the bottom of the vertical skewer where it extends beyond kite. Add a drop of glue to secure. Thread tail through this loop and secure with a piece of tape.

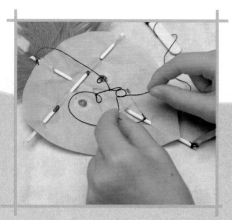

9. Glue 3 feathers to top of kite.

10. Tape the end of 5 or 6 yards of thread to a craft stick and wind the rest of the thread around the stick. Tie the loose end of the thread to the center loop on the bridle.

## Variation

Use different-colored bags and make different animal faces. Or, you can make a whole flock of birds.

# FLYING TIPS

If the kite hangs back and will not climb, move the flying thread to the top loop of the bridle. If the kite climbs too far overhead, move the flying thread to the bottom loop. You might have to make new loops and move the flying thread until the kite flies perfectly. If this doesn't work, trim the kite tail.

# CIRCULAR GLIDER

It's unusual and incredible! Circular wings work very well in propelling this glider through the air.

## WHAT YOU'LL NEED

6¼ × 1¼-inch cherry-red cardstock

Drinking straw

Adhesive stickers

**Tools:** ruler, pencil, scissors, transparent tape

1. Measure and cut one ¾×6¼-inch strip and one ½×5½-inch strip of cardstock.

2. Bend the longer strip into a circle and overlap the ends by ½ inch. Tape both the outside and inside edges to create a "pocket."

3. Pry open the pocket and slip 1 end of the drinking straw through the pocket.

4. Repeat Step 2, using the second strip of cardstock. Slip the other end of the straw through the second pocket.

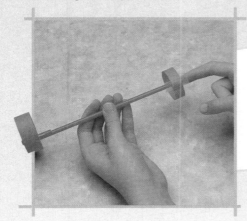

5. Position the 2 circles exactly across from each other on each end of the straw. Tape them in place securely. Decorate both circles with adhesive stickers.

## FLYING TIPS

Hold the Circular Glider by the straw, with the smaller circle to the front, and throw gently. If the glider nosedives, move the large circle forward slightly and try again. If the glider wobbles, move the small circle back slightly and try again. Watch what happens when you try to fly the Circular Glider backwards, with the large circle in front.

# STAR CASTER

THIS FLYING
SAUCER WILL HAVE
EVERYONE SEEING
STARS. DECORATE
WITH PAINT AND
STICKERS, THEN
CAST THIS SAUCER
UP INTO THE SKY.

## WHAT YOU'LL NEED

2 foam plates, 9-inch diameter
Acrylic paint: blue, turquoise
4 pennies
Adhesive star stickers

**Tools:** scissors, kitchen sponge, paint plate, paper towel, craft glue

**1.** Use scissors to poke a hole in the middle of each plate. Be careful not to stab yourself! Starting at the hole, cut out the middle part of each plate.

**2.** Dampen kitchen sponge and squeeze out excess water. Squeeze some blue paint onto your paint plate. Dip wet sponge into the paint and dab excess paint onto paper towel. Smoothly sponge the color on the top of each plate. Allow to dry. Turn plates over and sponge-paint the bottom. Allow to dry.

**3.** Repeat this process with turquoise paint, using a clean sponge to sponge-paint the turquoise paint over the blue only on the top side of each plate. Allow to dry.

**4.** Squeeze a ribbon of glue along the inside rim of 1 of the plates. Turn the second plate over and glue the 2 rims together. Let dry.

**5.** Place the 4 pennies along the outer edge of the top plate. Make sure the amount of space between each of the pennies is equal. Glue pennies in place. This will add weight and allow the Star Caster to soar through the air!

**6.** Scatter the star stickers in an attractive design on both plates. Make sure you decorate the inside of the saucer as well.

**Variation**

Use paper plates instead of foam and see if the Star Caster will fly farther.

## FLYING TIPS

Take the Star Caster outside, hold it by the edge, and give it a good hard sideways toss, similar to the way you might throw a Frisbee flying disc. This is a good toy to use with a friend in a game of catch.

If there is a breeze, use it to help loft the Star Caster. With the wind blowing against your back, see how far the Star Caster will fly.

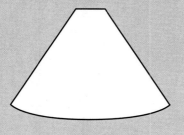

**Come Backer
triangle pattern**

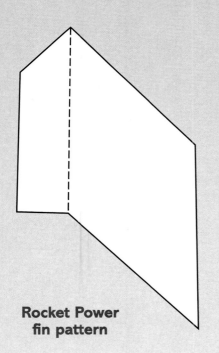

**Rocket Power
fin pattern**

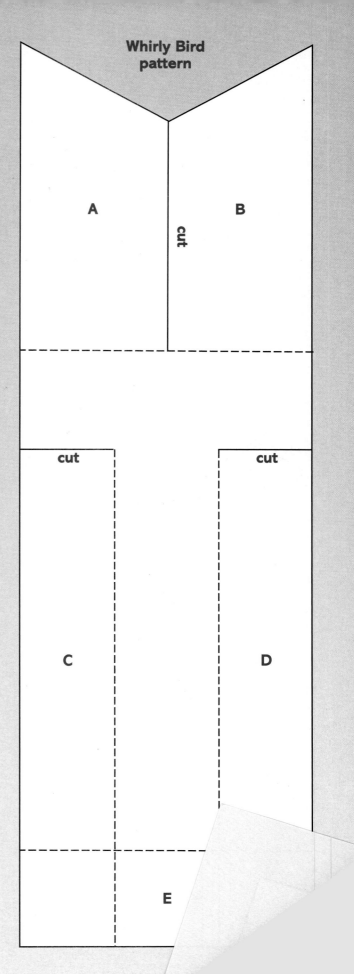

**Whirly Bird
pattern**

A

B

cut

cut

cut

C

D

E

47

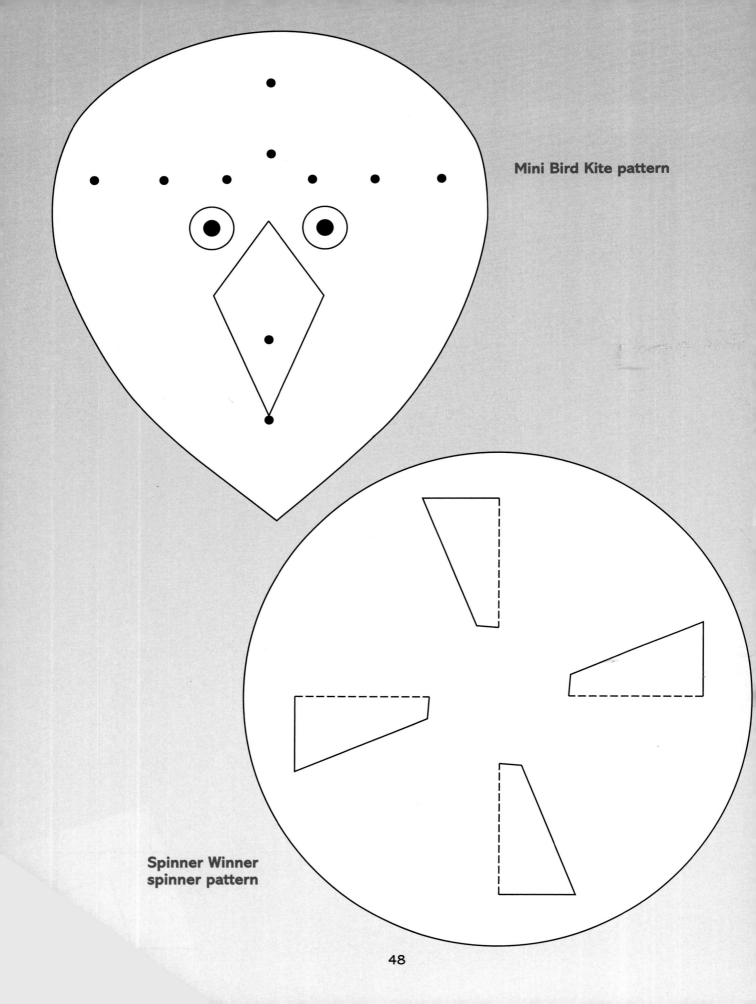

**Mini Bird Kite pattern**

**Spinner Winner spinner pattern**

48